COMMUNITY HELPERS

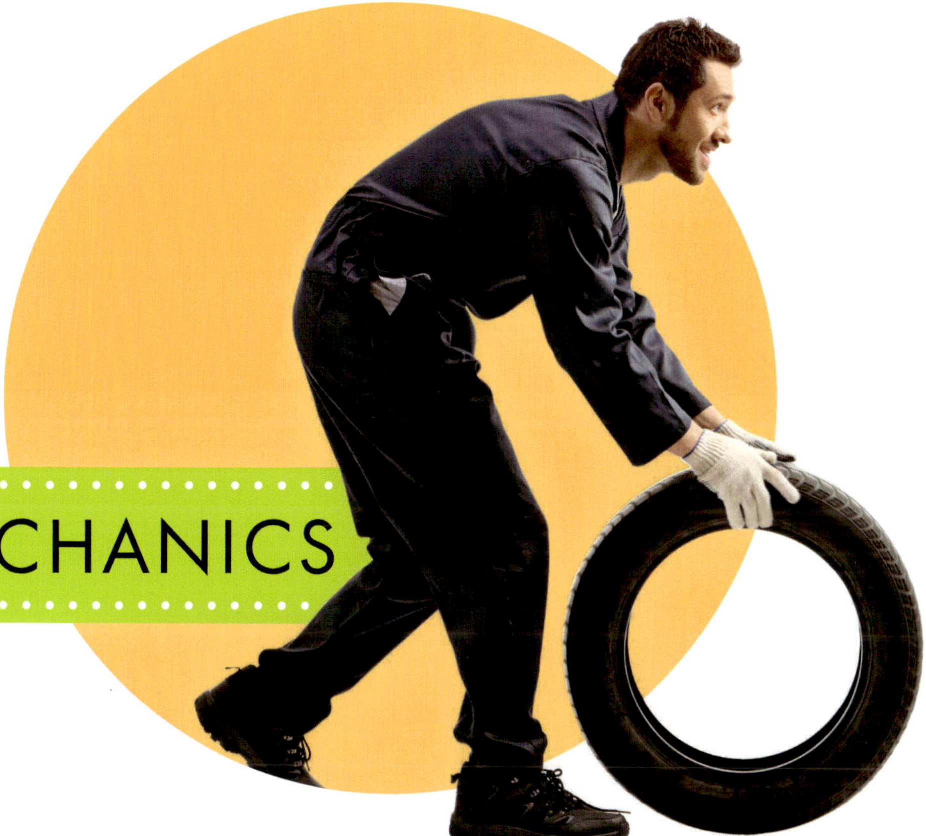

MECHANICS

by Golriz Golkar

repair shop

tire

Look for these words and pictures as you read.

battery

engine

Mechanics help us.
What do they do?

Oh no!
A car breaks down.
It goes to the repair shop.
repair shop

tire

The car is lifted.
The flat tire comes off.
A new tire goes on.

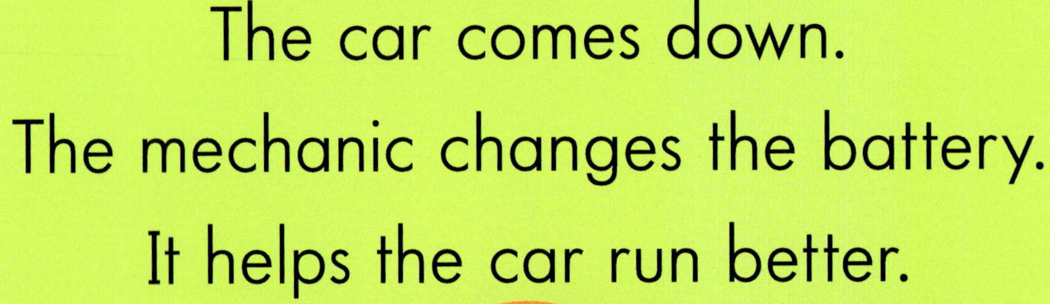

The car comes down.
The mechanic changes the battery.
It helps the car run better.

battery

Time to check the lights.
Front and back.
Left and right.
Blink! Blink!

The mechanic checks the engine.

Vroom!

The car is fixed!

Mechanics fix cars.
They help people get around!

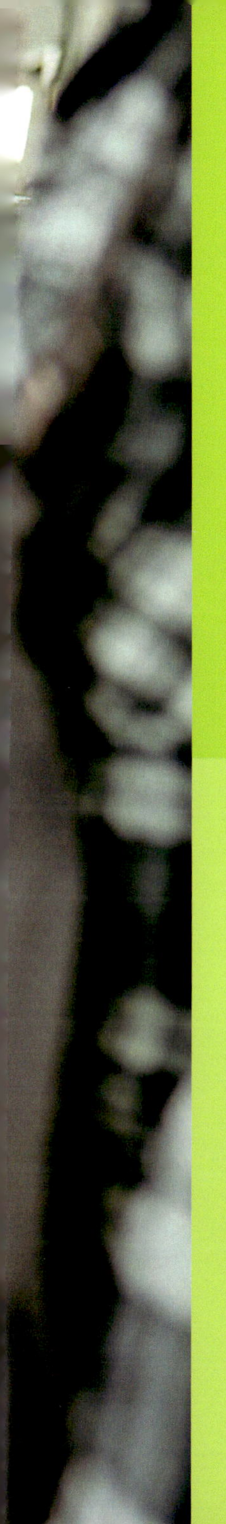

repair shop

tire

Did you find?

battery

engine

Spot is published by Amicus Learning, an imprint of Amicus
P.O. Box 227, Mankato, MN 56002
www.amicuspublishing.us

Library of Congress Cataloging-in-Publication Data
Names: Golkar, Golriz, author.
Title: Mechanics / by Golriz Golkar.
Description: Mankato, MN : Amicus Learning, an imprint of Amicus, [2026] | Series: Spot community helpers | Audience term: Children | Audience: Ages 4–7 | Audience: Grades K–1 | Summary: "Mechanics fix cars, change tires, and more. Learn how they help the community in this low-level beginning reader that reinforces new vocabulary with a search-and-find feature. A great early social studies book that will inspire kindergartners and first graders to learn about jobs in their community"– Provided by publisher.
Identifiers: LCCN 2024043687 (print) | LCCN 2024043688 (ebook) | ISBN 9798892004916 (library binding) | ISBN 9798892005456 (paperback) | ISBN 9798892005999 (ebook)
Subjects: LCSH: Automobile mechanics—Juvenile literature. | Occupations—Juvenile literature.
Classification: LCC HD8039.M34 G65 2026 (print) | LCC HD8039.M34 (ebook) | DDC 338.7/6292872--dc23/eng/20250105
LC record available at https://lccn.loc.gov/2024043687
LC ebook record available at https://lccn.loc.gov/2024043688

Ana Brauer, editor
Deb Miner, series designer
Sara Hood, book designer and photo researcher

Photos by Dreamstime/Industryviews, 10–11; Getty Images/Matthew Ng, 6-7, Yagi-Studio, 12–13; Shutterstock/f.t.Photographer, 14, LightField Studios, cover, Ljupco Smokovski, 1, Memory Stockphoto, 4–5, Roman Chazov, 3, Tong_stocker, 8–9

MECHANICS